# 50 The Best Dishes to Cook

By: Kelly Johnson

# Table of Contents

- Beef Wellington
- Chicken Marsala
- Paella
- Coq au Vin
- Beef Bourguignon
- Chicken Cacciatore
- Risotto
- Shrimp and Grits
- Tacos Al Pastor
- Sushi Rolls
- Lasagna
- Pad Thai
- Moussaka
- Chicken Tikka Masala
- Pho
- Ramen
- Jambalaya
- Fettuccine Alfredo
- Baked Ziti
- Ceviche
- Lobster Bisque
- Peking Duck
- Bangers and Mash
- Pulled Pork Sandwiches
- Beef Stew
- Chicken Pot Pie
- Baked Alaska
- Pork Schnitzel
- Beef Empanadas
- Grilled Octopus
- Eggplant Parmesan
- Barbecued Ribs
- Shepherd's Pie
- Chateaubriand
- Chicken Fried Rice
- Pappardelle with Ragu

- Tom Yum Soup
- Goulash
- Mussels in White Wine Sauce
- Clam Chowder
- Croque Monsieur
- Souvlaki
- Beef and Broccoli Stir-fry
- Tiramisu
- Grilled Cheese and Tomato Soup
- Croissants
- Ratatouille
- Carbonara
- Empanadas

# Beef Wellington

**Ingredients:**

- 2 lb beef tenderloin
- Salt and pepper to taste
- 2 tbsp olive oil
- 2 tbsp Dijon mustard
- 1 lb mushrooms, finely chopped
- 1 shallot, minced
- 2 tbsp butter
- 6 slices prosciutto
- 1 sheet puff pastry, thawed
- 1 egg, beaten

**Instructions:**

1. Season the beef with salt and pepper. Sear in olive oil over high heat until browned on all sides. Let cool, then coat with Dijon mustard.
2. In a pan, cook mushrooms and shallot in butter until all moisture evaporates. Let cool.
3. Lay prosciutto slices on plastic wrap, spread mushroom mixture on top, and place beef in the center. Wrap tightly and chill.
4. Roll out puff pastry and wrap the beef. Brush with egg wash and chill for 15 minutes.
5. Bake at 400°F (200°C) for 40–45 minutes until golden brown. Let rest before slicing.

## Chicken Marsala

**Ingredients:**

- 2 boneless chicken breasts
- 1/2 cup flour
- Salt and pepper to taste
- 2 tbsp olive oil
- 8 oz mushrooms, sliced
- 1/2 cup Marsala wine
- 1/2 cup chicken broth
- 2 tbsp butter

**Instructions:**

1. Pound chicken to an even thickness, season, and coat lightly in flour.
2. Heat olive oil in a pan and sear chicken on both sides until golden. Remove and set aside.
3. In the same pan, sauté mushrooms until browned. Add Marsala wine and chicken broth, scraping the pan.
4. Return chicken to the pan and simmer for 10 minutes. Stir in butter before serving.

## Paella

**Ingredients:**

- 2 tbsp olive oil
- 1/2 lb chicken thighs, diced
- 1/2 lb shrimp, peeled and deveined
- 1/2 lb mussels
- 1 onion, chopped
- 1 red bell pepper, sliced
- 2 cloves garlic, minced
- 1 cup Arborio or bomba rice
- 2 1/2 cups chicken broth
- 1/2 tsp saffron threads
- 1 tsp paprika
- 1/2 cup peas

**Instructions:**

1. Heat olive oil in a large skillet and brown chicken. Remove and set aside.
2. Sauté onion, bell pepper, and garlic until soft. Stir in rice, saffron, and paprika.
3. Pour in broth and simmer for 10 minutes.
4. Add shrimp, mussels, peas, and chicken. Cover and cook until rice is tender and seafood is cooked through.

## Coq au Vin

**Ingredients:**

- 4 bone-in chicken thighs
- Salt and pepper to taste
- 2 tbsp olive oil
- 4 oz bacon, diced
- 1 onion, chopped
- 2 cloves garlic, minced
- 1 cup red wine
- 1 cup chicken broth
- 1 tbsp tomato paste
- 1/2 lb mushrooms, sliced

**Instructions:**

1. Season chicken and brown in olive oil. Remove and set aside.
2. Cook bacon in the same pan until crispy, then add onion and garlic.
3. Stir in tomato paste, then pour in wine and broth.
4. Return chicken to the pan and simmer for 40 minutes.
5. Add mushrooms and cook for another 10 minutes before serving.

## Beef Bourguignon

### Ingredients:

- 2 lb beef chuck, cubed
- Salt and pepper to taste
- 2 tbsp olive oil
- 4 oz bacon, diced
- 1 onion, chopped
- 2 cloves garlic, minced
- 1 tbsp tomato paste
- 2 cups red wine
- 1 cup beef broth
- 1/2 lb mushrooms, sliced
- 4 carrots, sliced

### Instructions:

1. Season beef, then sear in olive oil. Remove and set aside.
2. Cook bacon, then add onion, garlic, and tomato paste.
3. Pour in wine and broth, then return beef to the pot. Simmer for 2 hours.
4. Add mushrooms and carrots, then cook for another 30 minutes.

## Chicken Cacciatore

**Ingredients:**

- 4 bone-in chicken thighs
- Salt and pepper to taste
- 2 tbsp olive oil
- 1 onion, chopped
- 1 red bell pepper, sliced
- 2 cloves garlic, minced
- 1 cup crushed tomatoes
- 1/2 cup chicken broth
- 1/2 cup red wine
- 1 tsp oregano

**Instructions:**

1. Brown chicken in olive oil. Remove and set aside.
2. Sauté onion, bell pepper, and garlic. Stir in tomatoes, broth, wine, and oregano.
3. Return chicken to the pan and simmer for 40 minutes.

# Risotto

**Ingredients:**

- 1 1/2 cups Arborio rice
- 4 cups chicken broth, warmed
- 1/2 cup dry white wine
- 1/2 onion, chopped
- 2 tbsp butter
- 1/2 cup Parmesan cheese

**Instructions:**

1. Sauté onion in butter. Stir in rice and cook until lightly toasted.
2. Add wine and stir until absorbed. Gradually add broth, stirring continuously.
3. When rice is creamy and tender, stir in Parmesan cheese.

## Shrimp and Grits

### Ingredients:

- 1 cup grits
- 4 cups water
- 1/2 cup cheddar cheese, shredded
- 1/2 lb shrimp, peeled
- 2 tbsp butter
- 1/2 tsp paprika
- 1 clove garlic, minced

### Instructions:

1. Cook grits in water until thickened. Stir in cheese and set aside.
2. In a pan, sauté shrimp with butter, paprika, and garlic until cooked.
3. Serve shrimp over grits.

## Tacos Al Pastor

**Ingredients:**

- 1 lb pork shoulder, sliced
- 2 tbsp achiote paste
- 2 cloves garlic, minced
- 1/2 cup pineapple juice
- 1 tsp cumin
- 1 tsp oregano
- Corn tortillas

**Instructions:**

1. Marinate pork in achiote paste, garlic, pineapple juice, cumin, and oregano for 2 hours.
2. Grill pork until charred. Slice and serve in tortillas with pineapple chunks.

## Sushi Rolls

**Ingredients:**

- 2 cups sushi rice
- 2 tbsp rice vinegar
- 4 sheets nori (seaweed)
- 1/2 cucumber, sliced
- 1/2 avocado, sliced
- 4 oz raw fish (salmon or tuna)

**Instructions:**

1. Cook rice and season with vinegar.
2. Lay nori on a bamboo mat, spread rice on top, and add fillings.
3. Roll tightly, slice, and serve.

## Lasagna

### Ingredients:

- 12 lasagna noodles
- 1 lb ground beef
- 1 onion, chopped
- 2 cups marinara sauce
- 1 cup ricotta cheese
- 1 cup mozzarella cheese
- 1/2 cup Parmesan cheese

### Instructions:

1. Cook noodles. Brown beef with onion and mix with marinara sauce.
2. Layer noodles, meat sauce, ricotta, and mozzarella in a baking dish.
3. Repeat layers, top with Parmesan, and bake at 375°F (190°C) for 45 minutes.

# Pad Thai

**Ingredients:**

- 8 oz rice noodles
- 2 tbsp vegetable oil
- 2 cloves garlic, minced
- 1/2 lb shrimp or chicken, sliced
- 2 eggs, beaten
- 1 cup bean sprouts
- 2 green onions, sliced
- 1/4 cup peanuts, crushed
- 1/4 cup tamarind paste
- 2 tbsp fish sauce
- 1 tbsp soy sauce
- 1 tbsp sugar
- 1 lime, cut into wedges

**Instructions:**

1. Soak noodles in warm water until softened, then drain.
2. Heat oil in a pan, sauté garlic, and cook shrimp or chicken.
3. Push to the side, scramble eggs, then mix together.
4. Add noodles, tamarind paste, fish sauce, soy sauce, and sugar. Stir well.
5. Toss in bean sprouts and green onions. Serve with peanuts and lime wedges.

# Moussaka

**Ingredients:**

- 2 eggplants, sliced
- 1 lb ground lamb or beef
- 1 onion, chopped
- 2 cloves garlic, minced
- 1 can (14 oz) crushed tomatoes
- 1 tsp cinnamon
- 1/2 tsp oregano
- 2 tbsp olive oil
- 1 cup béchamel sauce
- 1/2 cup Parmesan cheese

**Instructions:**

1. Salt eggplant slices and let them sit for 30 minutes. Pat dry and fry until golden.
2. Cook ground meat with onion, garlic, tomatoes, cinnamon, and oregano. Simmer for 20 minutes.
3. Layer eggplant and meat mixture in a baking dish. Top with béchamel sauce and Parmesan.
4. Bake at 375°F (190°C) for 45 minutes.

# Chicken Tikka Masala

**Ingredients:**

- 1 lb chicken breast, cubed
- 1/2 cup yogurt
- 2 tbsp lemon juice
- 2 tsp garam masala
- 1 onion, chopped
- 2 cloves garlic, minced
- 1 can (14 oz) tomato puree
- 1/2 cup heavy cream
- 2 tbsp butter
- 1 tsp cumin
- 1 tsp turmeric

**Instructions:**

1. Marinate chicken in yogurt, lemon juice, and garam masala for 1 hour.
2. Cook chicken in a pan until golden, then set aside.
3. In the same pan, sauté onion and garlic. Stir in tomato puree, cream, butter, and spices.
4. Simmer for 10 minutes, then add chicken and cook for another 10 minutes.

# Pho

**Ingredients:**

- 8 cups beef broth
- 1 onion, halved
- 2-inch ginger, sliced
- 1 cinnamon stick
- 2 star anise
- 1 lb beef (sirloin or brisket), thinly sliced
- 8 oz rice noodles
- 2 green onions, chopped
- 1/2 cup bean sprouts
- Fresh basil, cilantro, and lime wedges for garnish

**Instructions:**

1. Char onion and ginger over an open flame or broil until slightly blackened.
2. Simmer broth with charred onion, ginger, cinnamon, and star anise for 1 hour.
3. Cook noodles according to package instructions.
4. Place raw beef slices in bowls, pour hot broth over to cook instantly.
5. Garnish with green onions, bean sprouts, basil, and lime.

# Ramen

**Ingredients:**

- 6 cups chicken broth
- 2 tbsp soy sauce
- 1 tbsp miso paste
- 2 cloves garlic, minced
- 1-inch ginger, minced
- 2 packs ramen noodles
- 2 boiled eggs, halved
- 1/2 cup mushrooms, sliced
- 1/2 cup corn kernels
- 2 green onions, chopped

**Instructions:**

1. Sauté garlic and ginger in a pot, then add broth, soy sauce, and miso. Simmer for 10 minutes.
2. Cook ramen noodles separately, then drain.
3. Pour broth over noodles, then top with mushrooms, corn, green onions, and boiled eggs.

## Jambalaya

**Ingredients:**

- 1/2 lb chicken, diced
- 1/2 lb andouille sausage, sliced
- 1/2 lb shrimp
- 1 onion, chopped
- 1 bell pepper, chopped
- 2 cloves garlic, minced
- 1 cup rice
- 2 cups chicken broth
- 1 can (14 oz) diced tomatoes
- 1 tsp paprika
- 1/2 tsp thyme

**Instructions:**

1. Brown chicken and sausage in a pan. Remove and set aside.
2. Sauté onion, bell pepper, and garlic. Stir in rice, broth, tomatoes, and spices.
3. Simmer for 15 minutes, then add shrimp and cook for another 5 minutes.

## Fettuccine Alfredo

### Ingredients:

- 12 oz fettuccine
- 1 cup heavy cream
- 1/2 cup butter
- 1 cup Parmesan cheese
- Salt and pepper to taste
- 1/2 tsp garlic powder

### Instructions:

1. Cook fettuccine according to package instructions.
2. In a pan, melt butter, then stir in cream and garlic powder. Simmer for 2 minutes.
3. Add Parmesan cheese and stir until smooth.
4. Toss with cooked fettuccine and season with salt and pepper.

## Baked Ziti

**Ingredients:**

- 12 oz ziti pasta
- 1 lb ground beef
- 1 onion, chopped
- 2 cups marinara sauce
- 1 cup ricotta cheese
- 1 cup mozzarella cheese
- 1/2 cup Parmesan cheese

**Instructions:**

1. Cook pasta according to package instructions.
2. Brown beef with onion, then mix with marinara sauce.
3. Layer pasta, ricotta, and meat sauce in a baking dish.
4. Top with mozzarella and Parmesan, then bake at 375°F (190°C) for 30 minutes.

## Ceviche

**Ingredients:**

- 1 lb white fish (tilapia, snapper), diced
- 1/2 cup lime juice
- 1/2 cup lemon juice
- 1/2 red onion, chopped
- 1 jalapeño, minced
- 1/2 cup chopped cilantro
- 1 tomato, diced
- Salt and pepper to taste

**Instructions:**

1. Marinate fish in lime and lemon juice for 30 minutes until opaque.
2. Stir in onion, jalapeño, cilantro, and tomato.
3. Season with salt and pepper, then serve chilled.

## Lobster Bisque

**Ingredients:**

- 2 lobster tails
- 2 tbsp butter
- 1 onion, chopped
- 2 cloves garlic, minced
- 2 tbsp tomato paste
- 2 cups seafood stock
- 1/2 cup heavy cream
- 1/2 cup white wine
- 1 tsp paprika

**Instructions:**

1. Boil lobster tails, then remove meat and chop.
2. Sauté onion and garlic in butter, then stir in tomato paste, stock, and wine.
3. Simmer for 10 minutes, then blend until smooth.
4. Stir in cream, paprika, and lobster meat.

## Peking Duck

### Ingredients:

- 1 whole duck (4-5 lbs)
- 1/4 cup honey
- 2 tbsp soy sauce
- 1 tbsp Chinese five-spice powder
- 1 tbsp hoisin sauce
- 2 tbsp rice vinegar
- 2 tbsp cornstarch mixed with 2 tbsp water (slurry)
- Mandarin pancakes for serving
- Sliced cucumber and green onions

### Instructions:

1. Rinse and dry the duck. Prick the skin all over with a fork.
2. Mix honey, soy sauce, hoisin sauce, vinegar, and five-spice powder. Brush over the duck.
3. Hang or place the duck on a rack in the fridge overnight for the skin to dry.
4. Roast at 375°F (190°C) for 90 minutes, turning occasionally.
5. Brush with cornstarch slurry, increase heat to 425°F (220°C), and roast for another 15 minutes until crispy.
6. Serve with pancakes, cucumber, and green onions.

## Bangers and Mash

**Ingredients:**

- 6 pork sausages
- 2 tbsp butter
- 1 onion, sliced
- 1 tbsp flour
- 1 cup beef broth
- 1/2 cup milk
- 4 large potatoes, peeled and chopped
- 1/4 cup heavy cream

**Instructions:**

1. Boil potatoes until soft, mash with butter, cream, and milk.
2. Cook sausages in a pan until browned. Remove and keep warm.
3. In the same pan, sauté onions, add flour, then whisk in broth. Simmer until thick.
4. Serve sausages over mashed potatoes with onion gravy.

## Pulled Pork Sandwiches

### Ingredients:

- 3 lbs pork shoulder
- 1 cup BBQ sauce
- 1 tbsp smoked paprika
- 1 tbsp brown sugar
- 1 tsp salt
- 1 tsp black pepper
- 1 onion, sliced
- 4 sandwich buns

### Instructions:

1. Rub pork with paprika, sugar, salt, and pepper. Place in a slow cooker with onions and BBQ sauce.
2. Cook on low for 8 hours. Shred pork and mix with sauce.
3. Serve on buns with extra BBQ sauce.

## Beef Stew

**Ingredients:**

- 2 lbs beef chuck, cubed
- 2 tbsp flour
- 1 onion, chopped
- 2 carrots, sliced
- 2 potatoes, diced
- 3 cups beef broth
- 1 tbsp tomato paste
- 1 tsp thyme

**Instructions:**

1. Dredge beef in flour, then brown in a pot.
2. Add onions, carrots, and tomato paste. Stir for 2 minutes.
3. Pour in broth and thyme. Simmer for 2 hours.
4. Add potatoes and cook for another 30 minutes.

## Chicken Pot Pie

**Ingredients:**

- 1 lb chicken breast, cubed
- 1/2 cup butter
- 1/2 cup flour
- 1 cup chicken broth
- 1 cup milk
- 1 cup mixed vegetables
- 1 pie crust

**Instructions:**

1. Sauté chicken until cooked, then set aside.
2. Melt butter, stir in flour, then slowly whisk in broth and milk. Simmer until thick.
3. Add vegetables and chicken, then pour into a pie dish.
4. Cover with pie crust and bake at 375°F (190°C) for 35 minutes.

## Baked Alaska

**Ingredients:**

- 1 sponge cake layer
- 1 pint vanilla ice cream
- 4 egg whites
- 1/2 cup sugar

**Instructions:**

1. Place ice cream on top of sponge cake and freeze until firm.
2. Whip egg whites and sugar until stiff peaks form.
3. Cover ice cream and cake with meringue.
4. Bake at 500°F (260°C) for 3 minutes until golden.

# Pork Schnitzel

## Ingredients:

- 4 pork cutlets
- 1 cup flour
- 2 eggs, beaten
- 1 cup breadcrumbs
- 1/2 cup vegetable oil
- Lemon wedges for serving

## Instructions:

1. Pound pork cutlets thin. Dredge in flour, dip in eggs, then coat with breadcrumbs.
2. Heat oil in a pan and fry schnitzels for 3 minutes per side until golden.
3. Serve with lemon wedges.

## Beef Empanadas

**Ingredients:**

- 1 lb ground beef
- 1 onion, chopped
- 1/2 tsp cumin
- 1/2 tsp paprika
- 1/2 cup olives, chopped
- 1 egg, beaten
- 2 cups flour
- 1/2 cup butter
- 1/4 cup cold water

**Instructions:**

1. Sauté beef and onion with spices, then stir in olives. Let cool.
2. Mix flour and butter, then add water to form a dough. Roll out and cut circles.
3. Place filling in dough circles, fold, and seal with egg wash.
4. Bake at 375°F (190°C) for 20 minutes.

# Grilled Octopus

## Ingredients:

- 1 whole octopus (2 lbs)
- 2 tbsp olive oil
- 2 cloves garlic, minced
- 1 lemon, juiced
- 1 tsp paprika

## Instructions:

1. Boil octopus for 45 minutes until tender. Cool and slice.
2. Marinate in olive oil, garlic, lemon, and paprika.
3. Grill for 3 minutes per side until charred.

## Eggplant Parmesan

### Ingredients:

- 2 eggplants, sliced
- 1 cup flour
- 2 eggs, beaten
- 1 cup breadcrumbs
- 2 cups marinara sauce
- 1 cup mozzarella cheese
- 1/2 cup Parmesan cheese

### Instructions:

1. Dredge eggplant slices in flour, dip in eggs, then coat with breadcrumbs.
2. Fry until golden, then layer in a baking dish with marinara sauce and cheeses.
3. Bake at 375°F (190°C) for 30 minutes.

## Barbecued Ribs

### Ingredients:

- 2 racks pork ribs
- 1/2 cup BBQ sauce
- 2 tbsp brown sugar
- 1 tbsp smoked paprika
- 1 tsp garlic powder
- 1 tsp salt

### Instructions:

1. Rub ribs with sugar, paprika, garlic powder, and salt.
2. Wrap in foil and bake at 275°F (135°C) for 2.5 hours.
3. Brush with BBQ sauce and grill for 10 minutes.

## Shepherd's Pie

**Ingredients:**

- 1 lb ground lamb (or beef)
- 1 onion, chopped
- 2 carrots, diced
- 2 tbsp tomato paste
- 1 cup beef broth
- 1 tsp Worcestershire sauce
- 1 cup peas
- 4 large potatoes, boiled and mashed
- 1/4 cup butter
- 1/2 cup milk

**Instructions:**

1. Sauté onion and carrots in a pan. Add ground lamb and cook until browned.
2. Stir in tomato paste, Worcestershire sauce, and beef broth. Simmer for 10 minutes.
3. Add peas, then transfer to a baking dish.
4. Mix mashed potatoes with butter and milk, then spread over the meat mixture.
5. Bake at 375°F (190°C) for 25 minutes until golden brown.

## Chateaubriand

### Ingredients:

- 1 (1.5-2 lb) beef tenderloin
- 2 tbsp olive oil
- 2 tbsp butter
- 2 cloves garlic, minced
- 1 tbsp fresh thyme
- Salt and pepper to taste

### Instructions:

1. Season tenderloin with salt and pepper.
2. Heat olive oil in a pan, sear beef on all sides until golden brown.
3. Transfer to a 400°F (200°C) oven and roast for 15-20 minutes for medium-rare.
4. Let rest for 10 minutes, then slice and serve with garlic butter.

## Chicken Fried Rice

**Ingredients:**

- 2 cups cooked rice (day-old is best)
- 1 chicken breast, diced
- 1/2 cup peas and carrots
- 2 eggs, beaten
- 2 tbsp soy sauce
- 1 tbsp sesame oil
- 2 green onions, chopped

**Instructions:**

1. Cook chicken in a pan until browned. Set aside.
2. In the same pan, scramble eggs, then add vegetables.
3. Add rice and soy sauce, then stir in chicken.
4. Cook for 2-3 minutes, finish with sesame oil and green onions.

# Pappardelle with Ragu

## Ingredients:

- 1 lb pappardelle pasta
- 1 lb ground beef or pork
- 1 onion, chopped
- 2 cloves garlic, minced
- 1 can (28 oz) crushed tomatoes
- 1/2 cup red wine
- 1 tsp oregano
- 1/2 cup Parmesan cheese

## Instructions:

1. Brown meat in a pan, then add onion and garlic.
2. Stir in wine, let it reduce, then add tomatoes and oregano. Simmer for 30 minutes.
3. Cook pasta according to package instructions.
4. Toss pasta with ragu, top with Parmesan.

# Tom Yum Soup

**Ingredients:**

- 4 cups chicken broth
- 2 stalks lemongrass, chopped
- 3 kaffir lime leaves
- 2 tbsp fish sauce
- 1 tbsp chili paste
- 1/2 lb shrimp
- 1/2 cup mushrooms
- Juice of 1 lime

**Instructions:**

1. Boil broth with lemongrass, lime leaves, fish sauce, and chili paste for 10 minutes.
2. Add shrimp and mushrooms, cook until shrimp is pink.
3. Stir in lime juice and serve.

## Goulash

**Ingredients:**

- 2 lbs beef chuck, cubed
- 1 onion, chopped
- 2 cloves garlic, minced
- 2 tbsp paprika
- 1 can (14 oz) diced tomatoes
- 2 cups beef broth
- 2 potatoes, diced

**Instructions:**

1. Brown beef in a pot, then add onions and garlic.
2. Stir in paprika, tomatoes, and broth. Simmer for 1.5 hours.
3. Add potatoes and cook for another 30 minutes.

## Mussels in White Wine Sauce

**Ingredients:**

- 2 lbs mussels, cleaned
- 2 tbsp butter
- 2 cloves garlic, minced
- 1 cup white wine
- 1/2 cup heavy cream
- 2 tbsp parsley, chopped

**Instructions:**

1. Sauté garlic in butter, then pour in wine.
2. Add mussels, cover, and steam for 5 minutes until mussels open.
3. Stir in cream and parsley, then serve.

## Clam Chowder

### Ingredients:

- 2 cups clams, chopped
- 2 cups potatoes, diced
- 1 onion, chopped
- 2 cups milk
- 1 cup heavy cream
- 4 strips bacon, chopped

### Instructions:

1. Cook bacon in a pot, then add onion and potatoes.
2. Stir in milk and cream, then simmer for 20 minutes.
3. Add clams and cook for 5 minutes.

## Croque Monsieur

**Ingredients:**

- 4 slices bread
- 4 slices ham
- 1 cup Gruyère cheese, shredded
- 1/2 cup béchamel sauce
- 2 tbsp butter

**Instructions:**

1. Toast bread, then layer with ham, cheese, and béchamel.
2. Top with another slice of bread, spread butter, and grill until golden.

# Souvlaki

## Ingredients:

- 1 lb pork or chicken, cubed
- 2 tbsp olive oil
- 2 cloves garlic, minced
- Juice of 1 lemon
- 1 tsp oregano

## Instructions:

1. Marinate meat in olive oil, garlic, lemon, and oregano for 2 hours.
2. Skewer and grill for 10 minutes, turning occasionally.

# Souvlaki

**Ingredients:**

- 1 lb pork (or chicken), cut into cubes
- 2 tbsp olive oil
- 2 tbsp lemon juice
- 2 cloves garlic, minced
- 1 tsp dried oregano
- 1/2 tsp salt
- 1/2 tsp black pepper
- Wooden or metal skewers

**For Serving:**

- Pita bread
- Tzatziki sauce
- Sliced red onion
- Sliced tomatoes
- Chopped parsley

**Instructions:**

1. In a bowl, mix olive oil, lemon juice, garlic, oregano, salt, and pepper.
2. Add meat to the marinade, coat well, and let marinate for at least 30 minutes (or overnight for best flavor).
3. Thread the meat onto skewers.

4. Grill over medium-high heat for about 10-12 minutes, turning occasionally until cooked through.

5. Serve in pita with tzatziki sauce, onions, tomatoes, and parsley.

# Beef and Broccoli Stir-fry

**Ingredients:**

- 1 lb flank steak, sliced thin
- 2 cups broccoli florets
- 2 tbsp soy sauce
- 1 tbsp oyster sauce
- 1 tbsp cornstarch
- 2 cloves garlic, minced
- 1 tsp ginger, grated
- 1 tbsp vegetable oil
- 1/2 cup beef broth

**Instructions:**

1. Toss beef with soy sauce and cornstarch, let marinate for 10 minutes.
2. Heat oil in a pan, cook beef until browned, then set aside.
3. Sauté garlic and ginger, add broccoli and beef broth. Cook for 2 minutes.
4. Return beef to the pan, add oyster sauce, and stir-fry for another minute.

## Tiramisu

**Ingredients:**

- 1 cup espresso, cooled
- 3 egg yolks
- 1/2 cup sugar
- 8 oz mascarpone cheese
- 1 cup heavy cream
- 24 ladyfinger cookies
- 2 tbsp cocoa powder

**Instructions:**

1. Beat egg yolks and sugar until thick. Fold in mascarpone.
2. Whip heavy cream until stiff, then gently fold into mascarpone mixture.
3. Dip ladyfingers in espresso, layer half in a dish.
4. Spread half of the mascarpone mixture, repeat layers.
5. Dust with cocoa powder and refrigerate for 4 hours before serving.

# Grilled Cheese and Tomato Soup

## For the Grilled Cheese:

- 4 slices bread
- 4 slices cheddar cheese
- 2 tbsp butter

### Instructions:

1. Butter one side of each bread slice, place cheese between unbuttered sides.
2. Grill on medium heat until golden and cheese melts.

## For the Tomato Soup:

- 1 can (28 oz) crushed tomatoes
- 1 cup vegetable broth
- 1 small onion, chopped
- 2 cloves garlic, minced
- 1/2 cup heavy cream
- 1 tbsp olive oil

### Instructions:

1. Sauté onion and garlic in olive oil. Add tomatoes and broth, simmer for 15 minutes.
2. Blend until smooth, stir in heavy cream, and season with salt and pepper.

# Croissants

## Ingredients:

- 2 1/4 tsp active dry yeast
- 1 cup warm milk
- 3 cups all-purpose flour
- 1/4 cup sugar
- 1 tsp salt
- 1 cup unsalted butter, cold and sliced
- 1 egg (for egg wash)

## Instructions:

1. Dissolve yeast in warm milk, let sit for 5 minutes.
2. Mix flour, sugar, and salt, then gradually add yeast mixture. Knead into a dough.
3. Roll out dough, layer with butter slices, then fold and chill.
4. Repeat rolling and folding 3 times, chilling in between.
5. Roll out, cut into triangles, and roll into croissant shapes.
6. Let rise for 2 hours, brush with egg wash, and bake at 375°F (190°C) for 20 minutes.

# Ratatouille

**Ingredients:**

- 1 eggplant, sliced
- 1 zucchini, sliced
- 1 red bell pepper, sliced
- 1 onion, chopped
- 2 cloves garlic, minced
- 1 can (14 oz) crushed tomatoes
- 2 tbsp olive oil
- 1 tsp thyme

**Instructions:**

1. Sauté onion and garlic in olive oil, then add tomatoes and thyme.
2. Layer eggplant, zucchini, and bell pepper in a baking dish.
3. Pour tomato sauce over vegetables and bake at 375°F (190°C) for 45 minutes.

## Carbonara

**Ingredients:**

- 12 oz spaghetti
- 4 oz pancetta, diced
- 2 eggs
- 1/2 cup Parmesan cheese, grated
- 2 cloves garlic, minced
- Black pepper to taste

**Instructions:**

1. Cook spaghetti and reserve 1/2 cup pasta water.
2. Sauté pancetta in a pan until crispy, then add garlic.
3. Whisk eggs and Parmesan together in a bowl.
4. Toss hot pasta with egg mixture, adding reserved water as needed.
5. Finish with black pepper and more Parmesan.

# Empanadas

## For the Dough:

- 2 1/2 cups all-purpose flour
- 1/2 tsp salt
- 1/2 cup butter, cubed
- 1 egg
- 1/3 cup cold water

## For the Filling:

- 1/2 lb ground beef
- 1 small onion, chopped
- 1/2 tsp cumin
- 1/2 tsp paprika
- 1/4 cup olives, chopped
- 1 hard-boiled egg, chopped

## Instructions:

1. Mix flour and salt, then cut in butter. Add egg and water to form dough. Chill for 30 minutes.
2. Sauté onion and beef, then add spices, olives, and boiled egg.
3. Roll out dough, cut circles, fill with meat mixture, fold, and seal edges.
4. Bake at 375°F (190°C) for 20 minutes or fry until golden.

www.ingramcontent.com/pod-product-compliance
Lightning Source LLC
LaVergne TN
LVHW081329060526
838201LV00055B/2537